Circular Wal ~~g ~~~

Gritstone Trail
and Mow Cop Trail

Carl Rogers

Mara Publications

First published in December 1995 by Mara Publications, 22 Crosland Terrace, Helsby, Warrington, Cheshire, WA6 9LY.

All enquiries regarding sales telephone: (01928) 723744

ISBN 0 9522409 4 7

Special thanks to the following individuals for the checking of route descriptions: Jack and Audrey Rogers, Richard Evans, David Telfer and Martin Ogden

British Library Cataloguing-in-publication data.
A catalogue is available for this book from the British Library.

Whilst every effort has been made to ensure that the information in this book is correct, the author or the publisher can accept no responsibility for errors, loss or injury however caused.

Sketch maps based on the Ordnance Survey 1:25,000 map with the permission of the controller of H.M. Stationary Office.
Crown Copyright.

Printed & bound by MFP Design & Print, tel: 0161 864 4540

Contents

Introduction

Between them, the *Gritstone Trail* and the *Mow Cop Trail* form a long distance footpath of over 27 miles which take the walker through some of the grandest and most rugged terrain in Cheshire. In stark contrast to the gentle pastures of the Cheshire Plain which have come to represent the 'typical' Cheshire landscape, the eastern border through which these trails pass, is an area of high moorland, deep wooded valleys and rugged gritstone edges commanding extensive views.

This fine walking country forms the western limit of the Peak District National Park and is thus a popular and well walked area. As such the footpaths are generally well signed and maymarked although in the less frequented areas you will need careful route finding skills to stay on the recommended route.

The *Gritstone Trail* is the longer of the two trails covering some 18½ miles and like the *Sandstone Trail* further west, takes its name from the hard, underlying rock which gives the area its distinctive character. Beginning at Lyme Park on the outskirts of Greater Manchester the walker climbs quickly to the high moors which will his companion for much of the route. The distinctive gritstone edges of Kerridge and Tegg's Nose lead to softer ground around Sutton Common and Wincle Minn to finish at Rushton Spencer.

The remaining 8¾ miles to the hilltop village of Mow Cop are known as the *Mow Cop Trail* and form an extension not only to the *Gritstone Trail,* but also to the *Staffordshire Way.* From Rushton Spencer a rise is made to the gritstone outcrops of Bosley Cloud and Congleton Edge with their breath taking views of the Cheshire Plain, to finish at Mow Cop, famous for its mock castle ruins and from which the trail takes its name.

Location of the walks

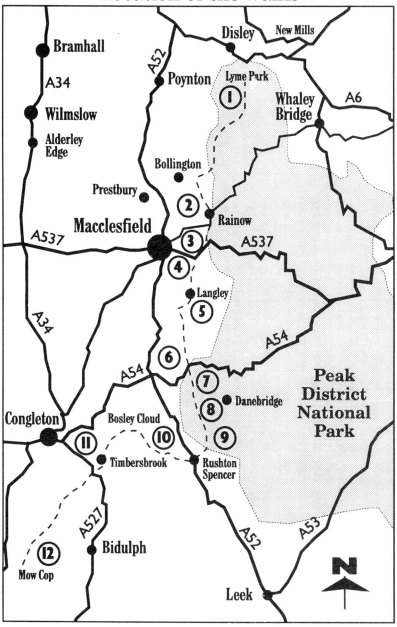

How to use this guide

Long distance walking on routes such as the *Gritstone Trail* and *Mow Cop Trail* is now very popular and numerous walkers will complete them in a single day. For many individuals however, such long distance walks are out of the question. Apart from the distance involved (about 27¼ miles for the two trails), motorists will encounter the added problem of returning to their car.

With this in mind the *Gritstone Trail* and *Mow Cop Trail* have been divided into twelve circular walks ranging from 4 to 7¼ miles, distances which the average walker should be able to complete in a leisurely half day. Those looking for a longer walk can simply combine two or more routes as required.

Alternatively, for those who want to complete the *Gritstone Trail* and *Mow Cop Trail* as a linear walk, the appropriate section in each chapter has been printed in underlined text. This will enable the walker to move easily through the relevant chapters as the walk progresses.

Maps

Although this guide contains all the information you will need to follow the walks, it is recommended that you take along copies of the relevant Ordnance Survey maps. These will help you to identify additional features along the way and will enable those not familiar with the area to locate the start of each route. Grid references and sheet numbers are given at the beginning of each chapter.

The Ordnance Survey publish two maps which are of interest to the walker: the Landranger and Pathfinder series. The Landranger maps are published at a scale of 1¼ inches to 1 mile and depict roads, towns, villages and woodlands. In addition, public rights of way information is shown in a red dotted line. Two sheets cover the *Gritstone Trail* and one sheet covers the *Mow Cop Trail*. A list is given below.

The Pathfinder maps are published at a scale of 2½ inches to 1 mile and show far more detail than the Landranger maps. This includes field boundaries, woodlands, farm tracks and buildings. These are the most useful maps for the walker and enable the exact line of a public right of way to be followed even where this is not visible on the ground. Unfortunately, the area covered by each map is rather more limited than the Landranger series which means that three sheets are required for the *Gritstone Trail* and two sheets for the *Mow Cop Trail*.

Pathfinder sheets:
    Gritstone Trail - 741, 759 & 776
    Mow Cop Trail - 776 & 792

Landranger sheets: 109 and 118.

The official symbols used to waymark both the Gritstone Trail and the Mow Cop Trail

CHAPTER 1

LYME PARK

Distance: *4 or 7 miles*

Section of the Gritstone Trail: *Lyme Park to Andrew's Knob.*

Start: *There is large car park at Lyme Park Country Park (grid ref. 963 823). Entrance to the park is from Disley. Grid ref. 966 843 (Landranger 109 &118, Pathfinder 741 &759).*

The Route

1. The *Gritstone Trail* leaves the main car park by a large wooden kissing gate at its south western end (to the right of a small play area). To locate this, stand with Lyme Hall directly behind you and bear half-left across the car park. Beyond the gate follow a rough track which rises gently to enter Knightslow Wood by a ladder stile adjacent to a second large gate. After a short walk through this attractive little wood you emerge onto the treeless expanse of Park Moor. Take the obvious path directly ahead signposted "Bow Stones". At the top of the rise a stile leads into a small field with a cottage to the left and a second stile takes you into a narrow lane. Turn left for a few yards to visit the Bow Stones.

These rather unimpressive looking stones are the shafts of Anglo-Saxon crosses which predate the Norman Conquest, possibly by several centuries. The reason for their remote position on this high exposed ridge is uncertain although one theory is that they mark an ancient boundary or frontier such as the northern limit of the Saxon kingdom of Mercia. Support for this idea exists in the name of nearby 'Lyme' which means 'boundary'.

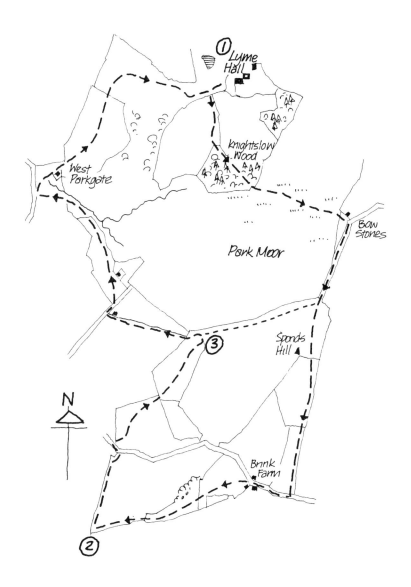

From the Bow Stones double back along the lane and after a few yards a gate leads onto a farm track. Follow the track along the crest of a rounded ridge with fine views westwards over the Cheshire Plain and east to the tors of the Peak District including Cheshire's highest point; Shining Tor, and Shutlingslow its most shapely summit. Where the lane runs into a large open field continue straight ahead on the obvious track (for the shorter alternative, turn right after about 150 yards, follow the right of way beside the wall on the right and continue from point 3).

A little further on the Ordnance Survey triangulation pillar on the summit of Sponds Hill can be seen to the right. This fine view point can be reached by a short detour although it must be noted that this is not a public right of way. Beyond Sponds Hill follow the track down to the road.

Just before the road you will pass a view finder on the left erected by the Council for the Protection of Rural England (CPRE) in 1975. This picks out highlights from the extensive panorama to be enjoyed in clear weather from these high moors and includes such distant hills as the Wrekin and Long Mynd in Shropshire along with the Clwydian Hills in North Wales. Nearer at hand, summits such as Shining Tor and Shutlingslow can be seen along with Bosley Cloud, Tegg's Nose and White Nancy on Kerridge Hill. On the Cheshire Plain the sandstone ridges of Helsby Hill, Beeston and Alderley Edge along with the massive bowl of Jodrell Bank radio telescope can also be identified.

Turn right along the lane and after passing Brink Farm and a stone house on the left, look for a signed path on the left. This leads you onto a well used farm track which cuts across the fields towards a small quarry. Just before the quarry bear half-left to a stile in the wall and make your way towards a group of trees to the left of the quarry mound.

Walk through the trees to a stile in the wall and join an access road for a few yards. Beyond a cattle grid bear left and stay beside the wall to the field corner. **For the Gritstone Trail continue from point 2 route 2.**

2. Turn right and keep beside the wall. In the far corner of the second field turn right and then left following the wall down to the road where a stile leads into a lane. Turn left and walk down the lane for about 150 yards to a large gate on the right. Go through the gate and bear right immediately following an obvious path which rises through a large grazing field to a stile over the wall. In the following field bear half-left and continue to rise. Where the slope eases the path bears half-right and after about 100 yards a raised path will be seen on the left.

3. Turn left here, or, if you are taking the shorter alternative turn right as you will be approaching from the opposite direction. Shortly the path bears leftwards and rises to a stile in the fence (ignore a stile just to the right of this in the corner formed by the fence and the wall). Beyond the stile walk straight ahead with a high stone wall to your right.

Again you are treated to a wide view across the Cheshire Plain with the tree covered escarpment of Alderley Edge and the airfield at Woodford being particularly prominent. Beyond this stretches the conurbation of Greater Manchester although from here there is little impression of just how densely populated this area really is.

This path eventually leads onto a track beside Keeper's Cottage, an attractive stone cottage on the right. Turn right here and follow the track past a small conifer wood to a signed footpath on the left. Stone steps lead over the wall and a well worn path cuts diagonally through the following field. Lower down the path dips into a small valley and crosses a stream before running beside the wall again. Stay beside the wall until the path takes you onto a narrow access track which eventually leads to the road beside the Methodist chapel. Turn sharp right here onto an unmetalled road which leads back into Lyme Park by West Parkgate. After the track begins to rise beyond the gatehouse, look for a gate directly ahead (the track bears left at this point). Climb the ladder stile adjacent to the gate and follow the obvious path through the field contouring the hillside. Pass through two gates on this path, the second leading onto a tarmac road. At a T junction turn left and return to the car park.

Lyme Hall is the largest country house in Cheshire and dates mainly from the eighteenth century when extensive alterations were carried out, although parts of the north frontage remain from an earlier hall built in the 1570s.

There has been an estate here since the Middle Ages when Edward III gave land at Lyme to Thomas Danyers for rescuing the banner of the Black Prince at the Battle of Caen in 1346. In 1388 the estate passed into the possession of the Leghs when Margret Danyers married Piers Legh. Family ownership remained with the Leghs until 1946 when Richard Legh gave Lyme Park to the National Trust.

The most impressive view of the hall is from the south where its portico of four giant columns supporting a massive pediment can be seen reflected in the quiet waters of the ornamental lake. This front is the work of Italian architect Giacomo Leoni and is typical of the Palladian style being developed during that period. Notable remnants from the Elizabethan period can be seen inside the house in a number of fine stone chimneypieces. Notable examples include the huge stone chimneypiece in the Stone Parlour on the ground floor and the elaborately decorated chimneypiece in the Long Gallery on the top floor.

Lyme Hall

The gardens and parkland surrounding the house are also of note. In addition to the lake there is a sunken Dutch garden and an Orangery built in 1862. The rolling parkland which surrounds this supports a herd of deer reputed to be the largest deer in the British Isles.

Lyme Cage, a square stone tower which can be seen on the hill above the road coming in from the main entrance and from the hills above the park, is also said to have connections with the deer. It is thought to have been built in the Elizabethan period and been used as a vantage point from which to follow the stag hunt.

CHAPTER 2

KERRIDGE HILL

Distance: *6¾ miles.*

Section of the Gritstone Trail: *Andrew's Knob to Tower Hill.*

Start: *Begin the walk in the village of Rainow. A few cars can be parked along Smithy Lane which leaves the B5470 just before the Robin Hood public house. Grid ref. 953 763 (Landranger 118, Pathfinder 759).*

The Route

1. Walk along Smithy Lane away from Rainow keeping right where the lane forks. The lane becomes rougher as you rise and eventually levels off with a wide view over the Dean valley to your left. At a T junction turn right and continue to the road by Billinge Head Farm. Turn left here and after a few yards turn right (sign) into fields bearing left almost immediately where the path forks to contour the slopes of Billinge Hill. As the path begins to drop ignore a track which bears sharp right to a farm lower down the hillside, instead, continue straight ahead over the wall and pass Winterside Farm on your right. Keep to the right-hand field edge now and enter a narrow lane by farm buildings.

Turn right and follow the lane to a farm. Pass through the farmyard to a little gate which leads down to a small footbridge over Harrop Brook. Beyond the bridge, bear half-right to a stile in the wall with a cottage to the left. Turn right up the access road and where this bears left after a few yards, take a footpath directly ahead which rises steeply beside a stream. Higher up where a stone wall blocks the way, bear left and zigzag through the trees to the top of the rise.

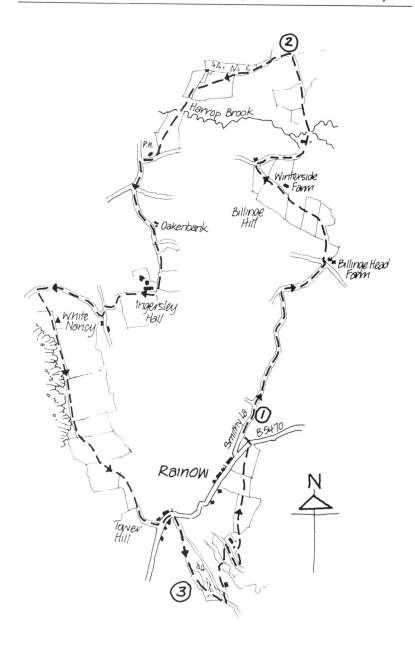

A stone stile leads over the wall here and the path keeps to the field edge straight ahead. At the head of the field climb over a stile and turn left along the wall.

2. In the field corner turn left through a gate and follow a descending footpath with a small beech wood to your right. Where the wall ends bear half-left through a large field crossing over a farm track with Berristall Hall to your right.

This stone-built hill farm was erected in the nineteenth century to replace the ancient half-timbered medieval hall of the Shrigley family, who were well known local landowners. The use of timber for building in this locality seems a little strange in the treeless landscape of today, but we must remember that oak woods covered most of these hills until the clearances of the late Middle Ages.

Lower down, cross a stream and turn left to a stile in the wall at the bottom of the field. Beyond the stile, descend the bank to a small stone packhorse bridge over Harrop Brook.

This picturesque little bridge survives from a period when the packhorse was the only reliable means of transporting goods through this rugged hill country. The absence of proper roads ensured the use of the packhorse until the end of the eighteenth century and many of our modern roads and bridleways follow routes pioneered by these hardy beasts.

Beyond the bridge cut directly through the centre of a large field. In the corner a stile leads over the fence and a short walk takes you to a quiet lane. Turn right along the lane passing the Cheshire Hunt Inn and at the road turn left. Where the lane forks keep left and go straight ahead at a small crossroads (Oakenbank Lane). Follow the lane past Oaken Bank Farm and where the lane bears left just before a stream, take the footpath straight ahead. Cross the water by a small footbridge and rise beside the wall skirting the grounds of Ingersley Hall on the right built by John Gaskell in the 1770s.

Just beyond the house look for a stile on the right and again keep beside the wall. In the corner of the second field steps lead down the bank and onto a track which bears left to a bridge over the River Dean. Continue to the road.

Turn left along the road and after about 100 yards turn right up the rising track to North End Farm. Ignore the turning on the left which leads to the farm, instead, carry on to the highest point of the lane. At the point where the lane begins to descend turn left onto a well worn path which rises steeply to White Nancy, the prominent folly crowning the northern end of Kerridge Hill which has been visible for much of the walk.

This distinctive landmark was built by the Gaskell family of nearby Ingersley Hall in 1820 to commemorate the Battle of Waterloo and at 920 feet, commands a fine panorama of the surrounding countryside. It was originally used as a summerhouse and contained seats and a stone table where visitors could picnic and find shelter. Unfortunately twentieth century vandalism has resulted in sealing up of the doorway.

The view from here on a clear day is extensive and takes in much of the Cheshire Plain stretching west towards the hills of North Wales. Eastwards the land rises rapidly to the treeless moors of the Peak District National Park.

To the north you have a bird's-eye view of Bollington, a small mill town based on the cotton industry of the eighteenth and nineteenth centuries. This industry flourished along the Pennine fringe where raw materials and a ready supply of the soft water essential to the textile industry were in good supply. The fast flowing Pennine streams also pro-

White Nancy

vided an endless source of power with the result that water mills soon lined the banks of every river and stream in the locality. In the village of Rainow alone there were over twenty mills. Thankfully these have now gone and the valleys are quiet and rural once again.

Signs of Bollington's industrial past are still to be seen with the two largest mills of the period; the Adelphi and Clarence mills, still dominating its narrow streets. They were built by the Swindells family who rose to prominence after Martin Swindell acquired the lease for the Ingersley Vale and Rainow mills in the early nineteenth century.

Follow the path along the crest of the hill beside the stone wall for about ½ mile.

The fine quality gritstone for which Kerridge has become famous has been taken from this hillside for almost 500 years and the Sycamore Quarry on your right is still worked on a relatively small scale to produce dressing stone and crazy paving.

Unlike most gritstones, Kerridge stone is very hard but splits easily along the bedding planes in a similar way to slate, making it ideal for roofing and paving. Many of the older buildings in Rainow and nearby Bollington have been roofed with Kerridge stone and its warm mellow colours line many of the towns pavements.

Just before the final rise to the highest point on the ridge, bear half-left onto the higher of two paths which cut diagonally-left down the hillside. This is just beyond quarry workings on the right. At the next stile you are again presented with a choice of paths; this time take the lower of the two. Just before a stream the path splits; a track continues the descent and a field path bears to the right. Take the field path identified by the *Gritstone Trail* waymark on the wall. Continue along the field edge and join a track which rises to the road (B5470).

To the left as you enter the track you will see the overgrown remains of Cow Lane Mill, one of over twenty mills which were built at Rainow when water was the chief power source. The viability of isolated mills such as this was destroyed when the Macclesfield Canal was built bringing cheap coal into the area.

Turn left along the road for a few yards before turning right into Berristall Lane, signposted "Lamaload Treatment Works". Beyond a row of cottages bear half-right onto a footpath which rises between fields at first then beside a small conifer wood on the left. **For the *Gritstone Trail* continue from point 3 route 3.**

3. About ¾ of the way along the wood look for a stile in the fence on the left. Walk diagonally down through the trees to the road, turn right and just before the cattle grid turn sharp left onto a field path. Descend the field to a house, cross the access road at the front of the house and look for a gap in the wall on the right. Bear half-left down the field now to a small footbridge over the River Dean. Beyond the bridge cross a small field and bear diagonally-left up the bank to a farm access road. Turn right along the road and just beyond a cattle grid turn sharp left towards the farm.

Keep right around the farm on a recent footpath diversion and turn right along a track on the left which soon leads into fields. Shortly the track forks; keep left and take a direct line through the following fields aiming for a small chapel. A gate between the chapel and a cottage on the left leads onto the road. Turn right for a few yards, cross over and turn left onto a narrow path between hedges which leads to Smithy Lane once again.

CHAPTER 3

LAMALOAD RESERVOIR

Distance: *5 miles.*

Section of the Gritstone Trail: *Tower Hill to Tegg's Nose.*

Start: *There is ample parking available at Tegg's Nose Country Park just off the A537 Buxton to Macclesfield road. Grid ref: 950 733 (Landranger 118, Pathfinder 759).*

The Route

1. Turn right out of the car park and follow the lane to the Setter Dog public house on the busy A537. Cross the road here and walk along the verge to the large millstone which marks the boundary of the Peak District National Park. Behind the millstone a stile leads into fields on the left and the right of way bears half-right along the field edge. The traffic is quickly left behind now and you are free to enjoy the wild Pennine landscape.

Cross a stile in the corner of the field and bear right to a small stream then keep left contouring the bank. Cut through the centre of the following three fields aiming just to the right of a group of trees on the skyline (stone steps and stiles mark the route). In the fourth field bear half-right into a larger field and, taking the same line, cross a gravel track to where stone steps lead over the far wall. Keep beside the wall now and after a stile and footbridge keep to the field edge again. About half way along the wall bear half-left onto a grassy track which leads to a gate. Go through the gate and drop to a small conifer wood which over looks Lamaload Reservoir.

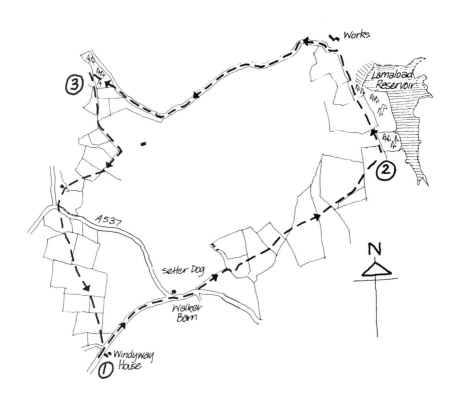

2. Turn left and follow the path beside the wood then cut through the following field to stone steps over the wall. Descend beside a young conifer wood to the water treatment works below the dam containing the reservoir. Turn left through a gate at the bottom of the slope and follow a rough track to a tarmac access road. Turn left here and follow the road for about 1¼ miles to a small wood on the left.

Across the valley you will see a rare remnant of the type of natural woodland which clothed these hills until the late Middle Ages. Much of this woodland was preserved by the

22

*existence of the Royal Hunting Forest of Macclesfield, cre-
ated by the Normans 900 years ago. By the sixteenth century,
however, pressure from the local population led to its enclo-
sure and the woods were cleared leaving small remnants such
as this only on land too steep for agriculture.*

Bear left into the trees and follow a narrow rising footpath to join the *Gritstone Trail* at the top of the hill.

3. Turn sharp left and follow the path through a number of
fields keeping the wall to your left. At a stile on the left
climb over the wall, turn right and continue with wall on
your right to a farm track (T junction). Turn right then bear
right again almost immediately onto a field path (stile) and
in the corner of the field go through a gate on the right.

The boundary of the Peak District National Park

Turn half-left now and cut through the centre of the field to a ladder stile which leads over the wall. Drop directly down the field to a footbridge over the stream. Turn right here then bear left up the bank to a stile in the field corner behind a holly tree. Continue up the field and after a stone barn bear half-right to the road. Turn left along the road for a few yards, then cross over and go through a gate which leads into fields once again. Walk directly up the field to a stile in the top corner.

To the right there are wide views across the Cheshire Plain to the sandstone ridges at Frodsham and Peckforton. Nearer at hand the distinctive outline of Jodrell Bank and the tree covered escarpment of Alderley Edge rise above this flat landscape. In exceptionally clear conditions the hills of North Wales can be seen on the far horizon.

In the second field bear half-left and follow the path (well supplied with stiles) through several fields finally dropping to the lane opposite Windyway House. Turn right and return to the car park. **For the *Gritstone Trail* ignore the car park and continue from point 1 route 4.**

At the back of the car park there is a view point and information board which gives an explanation of the distinctive Peakland landscape laid out before you. This view is dominated by the dark conifers of the Macclesfield Forest which clothe much of the steeper ground along with the conical peak of Shutlingslow on the skyline.

Steep hillsides and poor soil mean that the only viable form of agriculture in these hills is sheep farming and the Derbyshire sheep which can be seen dotting the fields are ideally suited to the harsh climate of the moors being highly resistant to the cold and damp conditions which prevail for much of the year.

CHAPTER 4

TEGG'S NOSE

Distance: *4½ or 6¼ miles.*

Section of the Gritstone Trail: *Tegg's Nose to Langley.*

Start: *As for route 3.*

The Route

1. Turn left out of the car park and follow the broad footpath (sign "Croker Hill 8.1km via Tegg's Nose summit") which runs parallel to the lane at first then between fields. Beyond the second gate bear left up stone steps and continue on the broad path which cuts through the spoil heaps of the quarry workings.

These workings provided good quality building stone, evident in many local buildings, until 1955 when they ceased production. In 1972 the site was opened to the public and designated a country park.

Further along the path there is an open air quarry museum with various items of machinery on display. Many of these seem extremely crude by modern standards but were surprisingly effective when in use. An example is the Jaw Crusher which was introduced in 1938 and used for crushing up to 100 tons of stone per day. Also on display is the Stone Shifter, a small crane like machine used to move heavy stone slabs. This particular one was used at the Sycamore Quarry near Kerridge for over 40 years. The Swinging Saw, built in 1920 was probably the most labour saving device used in the quarries and was capable of cutting stone into slabs at the rate of two inches per hour, far faster than by hand.

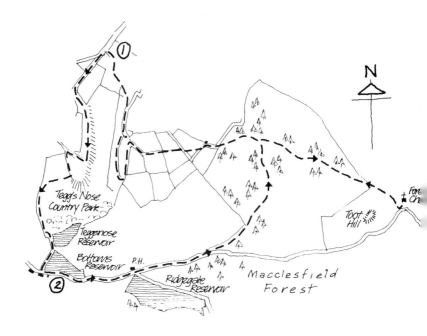

There are a number of paths through the quarry; keep to the most obvious broad path which runs along the left-hand edge of the workings before swinging right just before leaving the quarry area. After a short descent a broad fenced path joins from the left; turn sharp left here and after about 200 yards look for a stile in the fence on your right. Turn right over the stile and bear half-left down the field with a grand view over the Cheshire Plain directly ahead.

On a clear day, not only will you be able to identify the familiar outlines of Jodrell Bank radio telescope and the tree covered escarpment of Alderley Edge, but also the Peckforton and Clwydian Hills along with the tower blocks of Manchester backed by the fells around Rivington.

Immediately below lies the village of Langley with its two small reservoirs. Like Macclesfield its larger neighbour, Langley was once known for its silk industry and button making. It was also the home and birth place of Charles Tunnicliffe the wildlife artist.

The path is now broad and obvious as it descends steeply to Teggsnose Reservoir.

Enter a little car park at the bottom of the hill and turn right along a track which runs over the dam. At the far end of the dam go through a gate immediately opposite and a little to the left and drop to a footbridge before passing along the dam of a second reservoir. As you approach the lane bear left along the grass bank between the water and the road. A gap in the wall a little further on leads into the lane. **For the *Gritstone Trail* continue from point 1 route 5.**

2. Turn left and follow the rising lane towards Ridgegate Reservoir. Just before the reservoir bear left by the Leathers Smithy public house and continue until the lane levels off after about ¼ mile. Just beyond the track to Topclose Farm bear left again onto a rising forestry track with fields to the left.

As you enter the woods proper the track forks; keep right here, signposted "Walker Barn". Follow the track for some distance to a four fingered sign near the ruins of an old farm building.

For a longer excursion make a detour to the right (signposted "Forest Chapel") to the tiny hamlet of Macclesfield Forest and return to this point to continue.

The tiny church of St Stephen (Forest Chapel) standing at almost 1,200 feet, is said to be one of the highest churches in England. It is used little today except for the Rushbearing ceremony which is held annually in mid august and attracts a host of visitors.

The Rushbearing ceremony has been observed here for centuries and may have its origins in the practice of scattering the floors of cottages and churches with rushes, grasses and even sand in the days before they were paved.

On the hillside above the church is a site known as Toot Hill, an exposed location with a series of earthworks adjacent to the highest point. Although the name is of Celtic origin the earthworks are thought to date from the medieval period when a hunting lodge known as the "Chamber in the forest" is known to have stood nearby. At that time the surrounding land was part of the Royal Hunting Forest of Macclesfield, an area of land set aside for the exclusive hunting of the king and his barons. Agricultural activity was severely

Forest Chapel

restricted within the forest area and those caught in breach of its laws were severely punished. The name of Wildboar-clough, which came within the forest area, possibly recalls this period.

Alternatively, (or having returned to this point from Forest Chapel) bear left slightly following the sign to "Tegg's Nose". A little further on a three fingered sign ("Tegg's Nose") directs you half-left again and shortly you emerge from the woods into a lane.

Turn left down the lane and just beyond a large stone house on the right, turn left into a dirt lane for a few yards before bearing right where stone steps lead over the wall. Cut diagonally-left through the centre of the field to where a second stone stile in the wall leads back into the lane. Turn right here and after about 25 yards turn left into fields again. Keep beside the wall and in the bottom corner of the second field turn right along a farm track. Just before the farm turn left onto a second track and after about 40 yards bear right through a gate to make your way along the top of a grassy bank with a stream to your right.

Eventually the path drops to a stile which leads onto a broad path. Turn right here and cross the stream by stepping stones. Keep straight ahead now (ignore the stile on your left) rising a little and following the obvious path beside the wall which eventually joins a narrow lane with a farm to your right. Turn left here and follow the lane for about 200 yards to where a broad stone paved footpath bears left up the hillside. Follow this path back to the car park at point 1.

This recently restored footpath is known as Saddlers Way and follows the route of an ancient packhorse trail over the hills to Buxton.

29

CHAPTER 5

LANGLEY

Distance: *5¼ miles.*

Section of the Gritstone Trail: *Langley to Lowerhouse.*

Start: *There is a small car park at Teggsnose Reservoir situated at the end of Holehouse Lane in the village of Langley. Grid ref: 945 718 (Landranger 118, Pathfinder 759).*

The Route

1. Follow the track back across the dam and at the far end go through a gate immediately opposite and a little to the left. Drop to a footbridge before passing along the dam of Bottoms Reservoir. As you approach the lane bear left along the grass bank to a gap in the wall. Turn left along the lane and about 25 yards beyond the head of the reservoir, and just beyond the Ridgegate Water Treatment Works, turn right onto a farm track ("Throstles Nest Farm"), signposted "Croker Hill 4 miles".

Keep left where the track forks and continue to Throstles Nest Farm. Bear right around the garden and look for a stone stile in the corner of the field. Turn left now and after about 100 yards on the drive to Greenbarn Farm, bear right over a stile just before the outbuildings. Keep to field edges now and after fording a small stream take a direct line through the following fields before dropping into a narrow sunken lane. Opposite, rise out of the lane where wooden steps lead up to a stile and enter fields once more.

Cut directly through the following small field, pass Overhill Cottage with its small pond and take the track to the left of a large farmhouse. Continue through the farmyard and beyond the outbuildings take a rising track which leads to two gates. Go through the left-hand gate and follow the right of way beside the hedge at first, then bear left-wards and take a rising line through the following fields keeping above the stream to your right. Finally, make a rise to your right to reach the lane with farm buildings and a telephone box on the right.

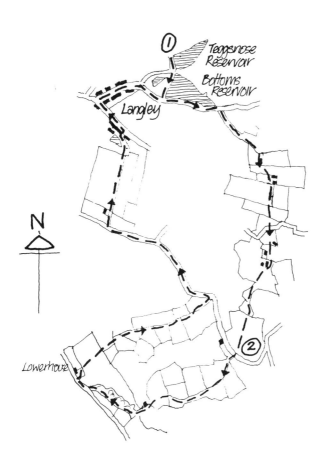

This landscape is typical of western Peakland. The peat bogs and moors of the higher Pennines are nowhere to be seen, instead grazing fields enclosed by low stone walls cover the hillsides and contain the familiar Derbyshire sheep highly resistant to the cold damp conditions which prevail for much of the year.

2. Turn right along the lane for a few yards, then turn left down a short track with a small farm building to the left. Beyond a large metal gate a farm track keeps left along the field edge. In the corner of the second field cross a stile on the left and continue on the opposite side of the fence.

After stone steps lead over a wall, bear half-left through the centre of a sloping field to a stile to the left of a small farmhouse. Pass the farm with a stream to your left and join the access track. A left turn left here leads over the stream and a stile on the right takes you into fields once again. Bear half-left through the field and, ignoring a stile on your left, follow the path through a small wood with the stream down to your right. At the end of the wood enter a lane beside a small group of cottages and turn right. **For the *Gritstone Trail* continue from point 2 route 6.**

After about 100 yards turn right into Lowerhouse Farm. Walk through the farmyard bearing half-right to a gate which leads into fields again. Cut leftwards up the bank (waymark on telegraph pole) and at the top of the rise bear right through the centre of a large field aiming for a stile in the far fence. Keep to the field edge now and after crossing a second stile on your right, rise to a third stile at the top of the bank. Follow the right of way along field edges until a stile on the left leads into the final field before the lane.

Turn sharp left and follow the lane for about ½ mile. At Brickridges Farm, (first farm on the right after first lane on the right) turn right down the drive and pass through the farmyard. A gate directly ahead beside the outbuildings leads into fields and the right of way keeps to the right-hand field edge. Cross a stile at the bottom of the field and after a foot-bridge bear left beside a small pool. After a tall metal gate bear right beside cottages to the lane. Turn left and follow the lane to Langley.

Langley was the birth place in 1901 of Charles Tunicliffe, one of the finest wildlife artists of the twentieth century. At the age of two his family moved to a small farm at Sutton Lane Ends a mile to the west of Langley and it was here that the young artist grew up.

His earliest drawings were inevitably of animals and his exceptional talent eventually won him a scholarship at the Royal College of Art in London. After his fathers death in the 1920s Tunnicliffe returned from London and settled in Macclesfield where he met and married Winifred Wonnacott, also an artist, in 1929. In 1947 they left Cheshire to live at Malltraeth on the west coast of Anglesey by which time Charles had established himself as one of Britain's foremost wildlife illustrators. His new home overlooking the vast sweep of Malltraeth Sands provided him with an endless supply of subject matter. He died at Malltraeth in 1979.

As you enter Langley turn right just beyond the church and follow the lane back to Bottoms Reservoir. Retrace your steps over the two dams back to the car park.

CHAPTER 6

SUTTON COMMON

Distance: *4½ miles.*

Section of the Gritstone Trail: *Lowerhouse to Wincle Minn.*

Start: *Take the A54 east from its junction with the A523 Macclesfield to Leek road. The road passes the Bosley Reservoir before climbing steadily towards Allgreave. Where the road levels off with the telecommunications transmitter on Croker Hill to the left, look for a small lay-by on the left. Grid ref. 940 673 (Landranger 118, Pathfinder 776).*

The Route

1. Walk east along the road for about 100 yards before turning left into fields, signposted "Foxbank". This is opposite a narrow lane on the right which runs along the crest of Wincle Minn. Bear half-right through the field to where a stile leads over a farm track. Keep straight ahead now with Tegg's Nose and the Macclesfield Forest directly ahead. In the following field keep right beside the old hedge line and join a grassy track which swings in from the right. Where this runs into a small field, bear left along the hedge and head towards Higher Pethills Farm.

A large gate leads onto the farm road and a bridleway sign directs you left towards the farmhouse. Just before the house turn right between the outbuildings to a small gate which leads into fields. Take care not to miss this. **Note:** the track which continues to the right of the house is not a public right of way.

The bridleway cuts through the following fields keeping close to the stream on your right to join the access road to Civit Hills Farm. This stands on the slope to the left above a small fish pool. Go through a gate beyond the pool and bear half-left to reach the track. Turn right and follow the track to the road (about ¾ mile).

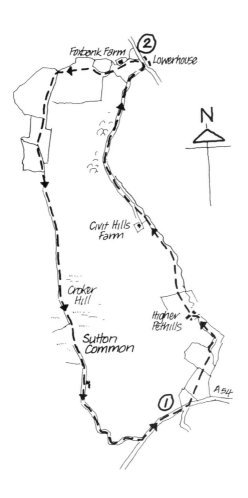

The masive transmitter on Croker Hill

2. Turn left along the road and after about 30 yards look for a footpath on the left, signposted "Croker Hill 2 km". This is now the *Gritstone Trail*. The path rises beside a small wood and at the top of the slope a permissive path keeps left beside the fence (the right of way passes through Foxbank Farm). Beyond the farm, keep straight ahead to a gate beside a small conifer wood. Go through the gate keeping beside the wall on the right and where this turns sharp right higher up the hillside, bear half-left through the centre of a large field to a ladder stile in the top corner.

Climb over the stile, turn left and follow the obvious path beside the wall for some distance. The path is easy to follow and is well supplied with stiles and gates.

Just before the final rise to Croker Hill, ignore a stile and the track on your right, instead keep to the left of the wall and only join the track when you are almost on the summit.

The view from here on a clear day is extensive and takes in almost the entire county. Out to the west the Cheshire Plain is laid out like a map with the familiar landmark of Jodrell Bank being particularly prominent. Nearer at hand the old mill towns of Macclesfield and Congleton sprawl at the feet of the Pennine hills, while to the east you will see the dark wedge of Shutlingslow and the fells of western Peakland.

From the transmitter follow the lane down to the A54, turn left and follow the road back to the lay-by at point 1. **For the *Gritstone Trail* walk past the lay-by and turn right into a narrow lane which runs along the crest of Wincle Minn. Continue from point 2 route 7.**

CHAPTER 7

WINCLE MINN

Distance: *5½ miles.*

Section of the Gritstone Trail: *Wincle Minn to Dumkins.*

Start: *Start the walk in the tiny village of Wincle which sits astride the River Dane on the Cheshire/Staffordshire border. Limited parking is available between the bridge and the Ship Inn part way up the hill. Grid ref 962 653. (Landranger 118, Pathfinder 776).*

The Route

1. Walk up the lane past the Ship Inn and about 50 yards further on stone steps lead into fields on the left. Bear half-right through the field to a stone stile and cross a farm road to enter fields again. Keep left beside the wall and in the corner a stone stile leads into a small wood. Take the obvious rising path through the trees and enter a field again at the top of the bank. Bear half-right through the field to enter a narrow lane on the right. Turn left along the lane passing Wincle Grange on your left and continue for about ¾ mile.

The Grange was originally owned by the Cistercian monks of Combermere Abbey near Nantwich and was built on land granted to them by Earl Randle Blunderville of Chester who built Beeston Castle in the thirteenth century. He gave them one caracute of land in what was then the Royal Hunting Forest of Macclesfield, an area set aside for the exclusive hunting of the crown. After the Dissolution, the Grange was sold to George Cotton and later passed into the possession of the Leghs of Ridge.

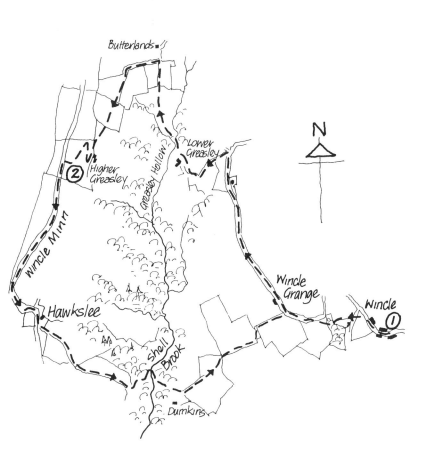

The present building dates from the fifteenth century and was built to replace an earlier grange on the same site. The stone for its building came from local quarries and it is though to be one of the oldest farmhouses in the southern Pennines. The monastic influence is apparent in its architectural details such as the long stone-framed windows in the northeast side.

The Grange looks out over the deep wooded valley of Shell Brook to the smooth skyline of Wincle Minn, once part of the estate granted by Earl Randle. To the southwest the profile of Bosley Cloud stands above the Cheshire Plain, while northwards the massive transmitter on Croker Hill presents the only modern intrusion into this ancient landscape. Higher up the lane there are fine views to right of the northern end of the Roaches and the hills around Gradbach and the upper Dane valley.

Where the lane bends to the right turn left onto a farm track, then immediately left again onto a second track which begins to drop beyond a cattle grid. Just before the farm turn right over a stile and cut through the field keeping to the right of the farm buildings. Beyond the farm cross a stile in the fence on the left and drop steeply into a wooded valley to where stepping stones lead over the stream.

A steep path zigzags up through the trees to enter fields again by a stile. Walk directly up a large field now following the crest of a grassy ridge higher up. At the top of the slope bear right along the skyline to a stile in the fence.

There is a lovely view from here back down the wooded valley of Greasley Hollow and Shell Brook to the rolling landscape of the Staffordshire Moorlands.

This lush valley is heavily wooded and a variety of trees line the steep slopes such as oak, beech, alder, holly and hazel. It was once part of the Royal Hunting Forest of Macclesfield, an area set aside for the exclusive hunting of the Norman kings and their barons. Almost all of this land has now been cleared and enclosed for agriculture but areas such as this, where incidentally you may still see a herd of semi-wild deer, recall earlier times.

Another reminder from the distant past can be seen on the slopes of Brown Hill to the left. On a tree covered mound just below the skyline stands Cluelow Cross, the stone shaft of a Dark Age cross similar to those at Sandbach and Lyme Park.

Climb over the stile and head towards Butterlands, a large hill farm directly ahead. Just before the farm turn left onto a track and at a T junction turn left again. After a gate there are two bends and then a straight section before the track bears leftwards. Take a direct line through the field here aiming for farm buildings to a stile beside a gate.

Bear half-right now to a second stile in the upper field boundary and turn left passing above Higher Greasley Farm. Just before the access road to the farm turn sharp right onto a zigzaging footpath which climbs the hillside to join the road which runs along the crest of Wincle Minn.

From this elevated lane you are presented with two very different panoramas. To the east stretches the gritstone landscape of western Peakland with the eye drawn inevitably to the shapely cone of Shutlingslow, the only real peak in the area; while to the west you have the wide sweep of the Cheshire Plain.

Lower down the lane you will come to Hawkslee Farm which was originally worked by the monks of Wincle Grange and came within their estate granted by Earl Randle.

2. Turn left and <u>follow the lane along the crest of the hill to Hawkslee Farm, about ¾ mile. Just beyond the Farm and immediately before a bungalow turn left onto a signed footpath which leads into a large field. Keep right along the field edge to a stile in the bottom corner. Cross the stile and keep to field edges eventually joining a farm track which shortly drops leftwards into the deep wooded valley of Shell Brook.</u>

At the bottom of the slope bear left and walk beside the brook to a small ford. This can be a rather tricky crossing in the winter when the banks are muddy. Once across the stream the path bears right up the bank then turns left at a fence and a short rise is made to a farm track. **For the *Gritstone Trail* turn right here and continue from point 2 route 8.**

Turn left over a stile and where the track runs into fields continue beside a line of trees which mark an old field boundary. Cross a stile in the corner of the field, bear right and rise beside the wall before bearing left to a stile in the field corner. Keep left beside the hedge to enter a narrow lane beside Wincle Grange. Turn right here and retrace the outward journey.

Walking towards the ancient farmhouse of Wincle Grange

CHAPTER 8

RIVER DANE

Distance: *4 miles.*

Section of the Gritstone Trail: *Dumkins to Barleigh Ford Bridge.*

Start: *As for route 7.*

The Route

1. Walk up the lane past the Ship Inn and about 50 yards further on, stone steps lead into fields on the left. Bear half-right through the field to a stone stile and cross a farm road to enter fields again. Keep left beside the wall and in the corner a stone stile leads into a small wood. Take the obvious rising path through the trees and enter a field again at the top of the bank. Bear half-right through the field to enter a narrow lane on the right.

Looking back there is a fine view to the rocky outlines of the Roaches and the distinctive pyramid of Hen Cloud backed by the higher moorland around Gradbach. The shapely peak of Shutlingslow lies to the left.

Turn left along the lane and just before Wincle Grange look for a stile in the wall on the left. Keep right along the field edge now and at the bottom of the field cross a stile bearing half-left to stepping stones over the stream. Just beyond the stream the right of way bends rightwards up the bank to run along the field edge.

After a short dip cross a stile in the field corner and follow a line of trees which mark an old field boundary. Where the trees finish continue straight ahead following the remains of an old farm track to a stile.

2. Beyond the stile follow the track straight ahead passing the ruins of an old barn on the right known as "Dumkins".

As you approach Barleighford Farm a sign directs you right onto a footpath diversion. A line of marker posts take you through grazing fields now to join the farm access road near Barleigh Ford Bridge. Turn right and follow the road over the River Dane to a second bridge which spans a narrow reed filled conduit. **For the *Gritstone Trail* turn right onto the signed footpath beside the conduit and continue from point 2 route 9.**

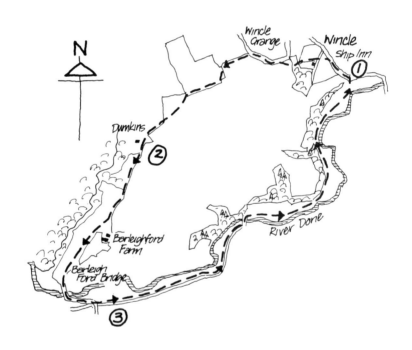

3. Turn left and follow a broad obvious path which runs beside the conduit for about ¾ mile. Where a large metal footbridge spans the River Dane on the left, cross over, turn right and follow the right of way beside the river for a further ¾ mile.

Just before the village of Wincle, turn right onto an access track by Pingle Cottage. Beyond a fishing pool on the left turn left over a stile in the fence and cut through a small field to a path which rises beside stone cottages. Turn right or left now depending on where you parked to finish the walk.

Wincle has a lovely setting; its cottages are gathered around the old stone bridge over the River Dane where it has carved a deep wooded valley on its short descent to the plain. On the Staffordshire side of the river is Swythamley Hall, perhaps best known for the wallabies which escaped from the private zoo kept by the Brocklehursts during the Second World War. Surprisingly they survived the bleak moorland winters remarkably well and were seen frequently over the following decades.

Just up the lane from the bridge is the Ship Inn, reputed to be one of the oldest licensed premises in the county. It was certainly trading in 1745 when a young man is said to have held the landlord and several locals captive for a number of days. He is thought to have been a Jacobite who had become separated from the army of Bonnie Prince Charlie and until recently an old musket hung on the wall which he is said to have left behind.

Another point of interest is the sign outside the pub which features a ship: Nimrod. *This was one of the ships in which Shackleton sailed to Antarctica accompanied by Sir Philip Brocklehurst who lived at nearby Swythamley Hall.*

CHAPTER 9

RUSHTON SPENCER

Distance: *6¾ miles.*

Section of the Gritstone Trail: *Barleigh Ford Bridge to Hug Bridge.*

Section of Mow Cop Trail: *Hug Bridge to Cloudside.*

Start: *Turn east off the A523 Leek to Macclesfield road in Rushton Spencer by the Royal Oak public house, then turn sharp left immediately and drive through the village. As you leave the houses behind there is a sharp right-hand bend; park on the verge here. Grid ref. 943 627. (Landranger 118, Pathfinder 776).*

The Route

1. Walk back towards the village for a few yards and turn sharp right into a narrow lane which drops to a stream. Just beyond the stream the lane bends right by a group of houses; continue straight ahead here and follow a farm track for some distance. Where the track bears left to a farm, continue straight ahead following a slightly better tarmac road which drops into the Dane valley.

2. Join the *Gritstone Trail* at the bottom of the hill where the road passes over a small conduit. Turn left onto a path which runs beside the water, signposted "Rushton 1.8 km". Follow this path for almost ¾ mile leaving the conduit at the third bridge where a waymark directs you right into fields. Bear half-left to a stile in the fence and cut directly through the following field to the main road (A523). Cross the road and take the path opposite, signposted "Mow Cop Trail, Staffordshire Way". This path shortly passes beneath

46

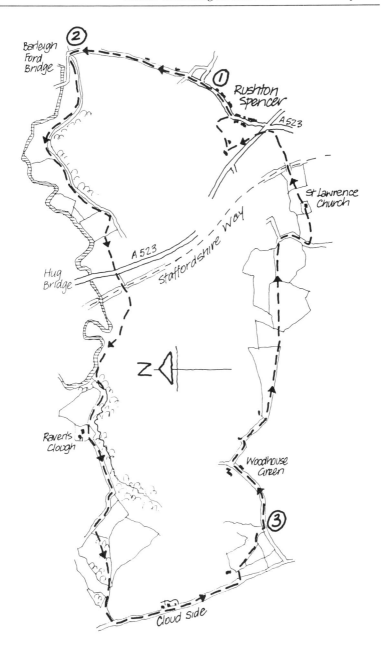

a disused railway to join the *Staffordshire Way* and complete the *Gritstone Trail.*

To your right the main road heads north to cross the Cheshire border at Hug Bridge, a corruption of "Hugh's Bridge". Hugh was a common name among the Despencer family who owned much of the land in this area during the Middle Ages and gave their name to the nearby village of Rushton Spencer.

The Despencers are said to have acquired their lands for services to William the Conqueror in the years after the Norman Conquest, particularly for the way in which they cruelly subdued the people of Macclesfield and Leek. They held their estates in what was known as "knight service" which meant that they had to follow the earl to war with a certain number of foot soldiers should the occasion arise. The occasion did arise several times during the Middle Ages with battles against the Welsh and in support of the Crusades.

The most notorious members of the Despencer family were Hugh Despencer, known as 'Hugh the Elder' and his son 'Hugh the Younger'. Both were unpopular favourites of Edward II and were said to have exerted a strong influence on him in his final years as king. They came to an horrific end in 1326 when Queen Isabella and her lover Roger Mortimer had them hung, drawn and quartered following a brief return to power.

From here the *Staffordshire Way* runs south to Rudyard Lake and the *Mow Cop Trail,* which is really an extension of the *Staffordshire Way,* continues to Mow Cop.

Beyond the railway bridge drop to a footbridge over a stream and keep right along the field edge. The route is rather indistinct here so keep parallel to the river until the field narrows and you are confined between woods on your left and the river on your right. A footbridge leads over Ravensclough Brook and a path rises leftwards through the trees for some distance.

At the top of the bank a stile leads into a small field with Raven's Clough Farm to your right. Pass through the field and turn left along the farm access road. Walk along the road with woods to your left and about 350 yards beyond a sharp right-hand bend, turn left over a stile into grazing fields. A well worn permissive footpath now takes you diagonally-right up the bank.

There are fine views from here looking northwards to Bosley with Macclesfield in the distance, and eastwards to Sutton Common, Wincle Minn and the Roaches.

At the top of the rise bear right over a stile and keep beside the wall bearing left to the road after about 200 yards.

The church of St Lawrence

<u>Turn left and follow the lane to the top of the rise.</u> **For the *Mow Cop Trail* turn right onto a rough track beyond a bungalow and continue from point 1 route 10.**

Follow the lane for about ½ mile and look for a footpath sign which directs you left down the driveway to Wood Common Farm. At the end of the drive bear right just before the farm onto a rough track which leads into fields. In the second field keep right beside the hedge and look for a stile in the corner which leads into a quiet lane.

3. Turn left and follow the lane to Woodhouse Green where a large farm and a small bungalow stand either side of the road. Just beyond this, turn right and follow a short access road. At the end of the road a well signed footpath leads into fields directly ahead.

Keep the hedge to your right and follow the right of way through several fields to a small pond. Climb over a stile to the left of the pond and cut directly through the following field. In the next field keep left beside the hedge until a stile on the left leads into a narrow lane. Turn right and follow the lane to St. Lawrence Church. Turn left down the driveway to the church and pass through the little cemetery.

This picturesque church with its large wooden bellcote and ancient gravestones stands on a slight rise isolated from the village of Rushton Spencer which it serves. One explanation for this strange hilltop location is the possibility that the church was founded on a pagan site. Evidence for this may be seen in the legend of "Satan's Stone", a large stone which originally lay in one of the nearby fields. This stone, said to have been rolled down the hill by the Devil may have formed part of a pagan monument along with two large stones which still stand near the entrance.

In the overgrown cemetery there are numerous old grave-stones from the eighteenth and nineteenth centuries, with the earliest being that of Thomas Godfellow, dated 1610, which stands just before the doorway.

Steps and a gate lead out of the cemetery and a well worn footpath cuts through the following fields to Rushton Spencer passing over the *Staffordshire Way*. At the road cross over and take the path opposite which runs beside a conduit. At the first bridge turn right and walk up the drive to a large farmhouse. Walk through the yard and look for a gate on the right behind the house which leads into fields again. Turn left along field edges and follow the obvious footpath to a footbridge over a stream. Turn right just beyond the bridge, pass through a little valley and rise to the lane. Turn left at the lane and return to point 1.

CHAPTER 10

BOSLEY CLOUD

Distance: *5½ miles.*

Section of the Mow Cop Trail: *Cloudside to Timbersbrook.*

Start: *There is room for a few cars in a small lay-by part way along Cloudside, a lane which runs along the northeastern side of The Cloud. This can be reached by turning left into Cloudside from Dial Lane between Congleton and Rushton Spencer. Grid ref: 908 634 (Landranger 118, Pathfinder 776).*

The Route

1. A rough track leaves the lane near a bungalow on the left (on the right if you are on the *Mow Cop Trail*). Follow the track and just beyond a sharp left-hand bend turn right up a flight of steps, signposted "Cloud summit". A short walk across the open hillside leads to the summit marked by the usual Ordnance Survey triangulation pillar.

This gritstone ridge is the last high ground of the Pennine hills. From here the land falls dramatically to the flat expanse of the Cheshire Plain and you are treated to a wide panorama in all directions.

To the west the Cheshire Plain is laid out like a vast green carpet, dotted with trees, villages and the occasional larger town. On a clear day the Clwydian Hills will be visible on the farthest horizon, while nearer at hand looms the massive radio telescope of Jodrell Bank which has dominated the landscape of eastern Cheshire ever since its construction in 1957. Closer still are the ten arches of the North Rode Railway Viaduct which provide a landmark from an earlier age.

Stone for the construction of the viaduct as well as the nearby Macclesfield Canal was quarried from the steep slopes below us. Prior to this a number of strange rock formations stood out from the hillside and were so distinctive that they each had names: Sugar Rock, the Raven, Mareback and the largest and most well known, Bully Thrumble which stood almost 70 feet high.

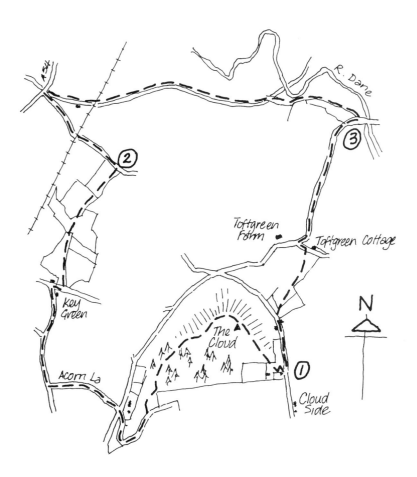

On the exposed summit of Bosley Cloud

To the east the view is very different. Cheshire's gentle green pastures come to an abrupt end on the slopes of Sutton Common and Wincle Minn. The familiar cattle and hedgerows are quickly replaced by drystone walls and hardy Derbyshire sheep. On Croker Hill stands the huge telecommunications transmitter with the dark wedge of Shutlingslow behind. Further south the distinctive gritstone edges of the Roaches and Hen Cloud reel away into Staffordshire.

Beyond the triangulation pillar the path runs along the edge of the steep hillside to enter a small conifer wood. Beyond the woods bear right at a T junction and continue to join a gravel track beside houses (Gooseberry Lane). Follow the lane as it descends to Cloudside. Cross the road at the end of the lane and continue along Acorn Lane, once part of an old route over The Cloud. At the bottom of the lane turn right **(For the *Mow Cop Trail* turn left here and continue from point 1 route 11)** and follow the road to Key Green.

Turn right at a T junction into Pedley Lane and after a few yards take a footpath on the left, signposted "Peover Lane". This path takes a more or less direct line through several fields well supplied with stiles.

2. Turn left into a quiet lane and follow this for some distance to meet the A54 at its crossing with the Macclesfield Canal. Turn right over the bridge and then bear right onto the tow path. Follow the tow path for about 1 mile.

The Macclesfield Canal, which joins Marple in the north with Hall Green near Kidsgrove, was designed by Thomas Telford and completed in 1831. It enjoyed a brief period of heavy use before it was replaced by the railways little more than a few decades later. Its most notable features are the twenty-arch aqueduct which spans the River Dane and the line of twelve locks which enable it to drop over 100 feet in less than a mile.

At bridge number 57 (number plate on the far side) leave the tow path and join a track which crosses over the bridge before descending steeply to cross a stile near a bend in the River Dane. Bear right now and keep beside the fence which also marks the Cheshire/Staffordshire boundary to meet a lane.

3. Turn right and follow the rising lane for some distance. Just before Toftgreen Farm, and directly below The Cloud, turn left into a narrow lane and after about 20 yards cross a stile on the right opposite Toftgreen Cottage. Bear half-left now and ascend the sloping field following the left-hand field boundary. At the top of the field enter a lane beside a small cottage, turn left and return to point 1.

CHAPTER 11

TIMBERSBROOK

Distance: *5½ miles.*

Section of the Mow Cop Trail: *Timbersbrook to Whitemore Farm.*

Start: *Begin the walk at the small picnic area situated in Weathercock Lane, Timbersbrook. Grid ref 894 628 (Landranger 118, Pathfinder 776 & 792).*

The Route

1. Turn right out of the car park and walk down the lane. Immediately beyond the bridge turn left (if you are completing *Mow Cop Trail* you will be approaching from the opposite direction so turn right immediately before the bridge) down an access road, signposted, "Brookhouse Lane". Walk past the house on your right and keep left by old mill buildings following waymarks to a small wooden footbridge over the stream. Beyond the stream a stile leads into fields. Cut directly through the first two fields following the stiles then, in the third field, bear right around the field edge to a stile in the far right-hand corner. Cut directly through the following field to a gap in the wall and walk beside a garden to enter Brookhouse Lane.

Turn right along the lane and after about 75 yards take the signed footpath on the left ("Bath Vale 1m"). Pass through a farmyard at first, then enter a short track which leads into fields. Keep to the right-hand field edge and at the bottom of the field bear left along the hedge ignoring a stile in the corner. After 100 yards or so a stile on the right leads onto the bed of a disused railway line.

This was the Bidulph branch of the North Stafordshire Railway which closed in the early 1960s and has now been turned into a public recreational route known as the 'Biddulph Valley Way'.

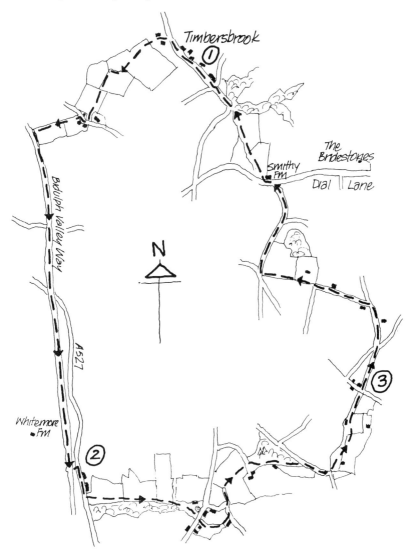

Follow the old track bed over Reades Lane and the A527 Bidulph Road. Just beyond this a sign welcomes you to the *Bidulph Valley Way* and you enter a more wooded section. Continue for almost ¾ mile and look for waymarks (*Saffordshire Way and Mow Cop Trail*) on the left directing you down steps to a farm access road. **For the *Mow Cop Trail* turn right and walk up the access road for about 500 yards to Whitemore Farm (on your right). About 200 yards beyond the farm the track bends right and there is a stile on the left. Cross the stile and continue from point 3 route 12.**

2. Turn left and at the main road (A527) turn right. Follow the road for about 250 yards and just beyond houses look for a signed footpath on the left. A footbridge takes you over the stream and into a large field. Walk directly up the field to a stile in the fence and in the following two fields keep right beside a small wood. Go through a gate in the top right-hand corner of the third field and join a track which bears right just before a house to cross over a dam which holds a small pool. At the road turn right.

Walk along the road for a few yards to The Talbot public house. Cross the road here and look for a stile at the back of the car park which marks the start of the public footpath. Keep left in a small playing field to a stile and sign in the top corner. Bear left past a stone house and at Hurst Lane turn left. Where the lane bends left after a few yards, turn right and follow a narrower lane which shortly runs into fields at a large gate. There are two stiles here; take the right-hand stile and bear half-right across the field to an iron gate beneath horse chestnut trees. Cross the drive to a large stone house on your right taking the path directly opposite and after a finger post keep right on a well worn path beside a stone wall.

At a farm road turn right and walk past the farm to enter fields again at a small stone stile with a wood to the left.

At the next fence turn left over the wall and continue to the road (with the wall on your right). Turn right along the lane and where the lane bends sharp right, bear left up the drive to "Glea Glow Cottage". After about 15 yards turn left onto a signed footpath and walk through a small field with a line of rocks on the left to a small stone stile in the far corner. Immediately beyond the stile bear right over the rocks beside the wall and cut diagonally-left through the field aiming for a small ruined cottage a short distance away. The

The Bridestones

right of way passes to the left of the ruins before rising to a large stone house. Bear right down the drive to the lane.

3. Directly opposite, a bridleway runs between fields with a fine view northeast to the rocky crests of the Roaches and the dark cone of Shutlingslow. At a crossroads go straight ahead and after about 300 yards look for a signed footpath on the left. Follow the path past a farm on the right and where a driveway comes in from the left, turn right into the garden of a house. Turn left immediately and keep to the garden edge to enter fields again at a stile in the bottom corner.

As you walk down the fields you are treated to a wide panorama of the Cheshire Plain with features such as Jodrell Bank radio telescope and the Mid Cheshire Ridge clearly visible. To the southwest the view is dominated by the gritstone ridge of Congleton Edge with the fake castle ruins at Mow Cop crowning its highest point.

Walk down the hillside now keeping to field edges until you can enter a farm lane by a stile in the bottom corner of the field. Turn right along the lane keeping left at a fork and at a T junction turn left. Walk down the road and look for a signed footpath on the right immediately after Smithy Farm.

Just up the road from here are to be found the remains of an extensive Bronze Age burial chamber known as The Bridestones. Although today only a few stones remain, they do provide us with one of the earliest signs of permanent settlement in this part of Britain. The stones originally formed part of a central chamber which, along with two lateral chambers removed in the eighteenth century, would have been roofed over with large stone slabs and covered by a mound of earth and rubble some 300 feet long and over 40 feet wide.

60

From studies made elsewhere it has been determined that chambers such as this were not only used as burial sites but also as territorial markers and religious centres. This is confirmed by excavations made in 1936-7 when a few flint scrapers were found but no bones. It seems that only selected bones, such as skulls and femurs, were interred after the body had been allowed to decay naturally. It is also thought that the chambers were in use for long periods before they were finally sealed up and covered with earth. The burial of the dead in this way clearly demonstrates the builders belief in an after life.

The present ruinous state of this once great monument can not be explained merely by its antiquity. Contemporary accounts from earlier centuries describe additional chambers circled by rings of standing stones. So what happened? Shortly after Congleton's first silk mill opened, a group of merchants and landowners formed a turnpike company with the aim of improving the Congleton-Ashborne-Derby road and thus speed up the transport of goods. The first section of this road made its way over Bosley Cloud and is now called Dial Lane (the road we have just left). To encourage turnpike companies to build and improve new roads an Act of Parliament was passed which gave them rights to remove stone and sand as required from any nearby common land. Unfortunately The Bridestones were too close to the new road to escape the builders attention and many of its stones ended up as foundation material. The rocks that remain were presumably too large to be of any use.

Keep left in the following fields with trees and a small stream to your left. Lower down where the field narrows enter the trees and cross the stream by stepping stones. Rise diagonally-left through a small field to enter the lane and turn right. Follow the lane back to Timbersbrook and at the crossroads go straight ahead returning to point 1.

CHAPTER 12

MOW COP

Distance: *7¼ miles*

Section of the Mow Cop Trail: *Whitemore Farm to Mow Cop.*

Start: *There is ample parking available on National Trust land below the castle in the village of Mow Cop. Grid ref. 857 574. (Landranger 118, Pathfinder 776 & 792).*

The Route

1. From the car park take the prominent path which passes beneath and to the left of the castle (when facing the castle).

This mock ruin, which stands on the county boundary, was built in 1754 by Randle Wilbraham to improve the view from Rode Hall, over three miles away on the plain. The tower was originally roofed and was used as a summerhouse by the Wilbrahams and the Sneyds of Keele who owned the land on the Staffordshire side.

In the early years of the following century the land around the castle became famous as the birth place of the Primitive Methodist movement. This was begun by two local men who decided to reawaken religious fervour by holding 'camp meetings', popular in America at the time. Although the movement was well supported, it was not popular with traditional Methodists who gave the new adherents the nickname 'Ranters'. Their first meeting is commemorated by a stone at the top of the car park.

Follow the track past the castle and just before a large house bear left through a gap in the fence onto a path with

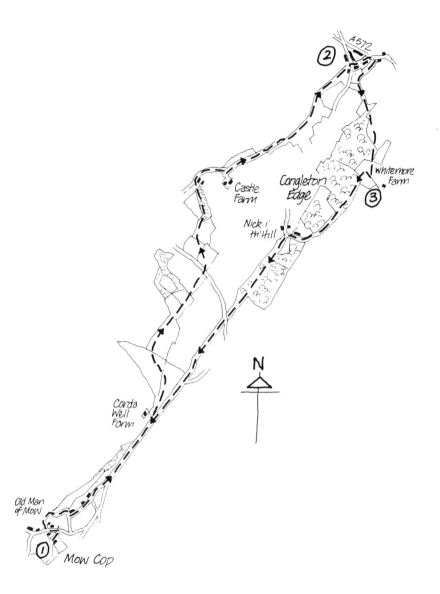

fields to the right. At the road (Castle Road) turn left and walk up the hill. About 100 yards after the road (Wood Street) begins to descend, look for a signed footpath on the right ("South Cheshire Way, Grindley Brook 52 km"). The right of way follows a track which bears left just before a bunga-low (La Ronde) to pass the Old Man of Mow, a 70 foot finger of rock on the right left behind by quarrying activity during the last century.

Stay on the track which a little further on bears sharp right just before a telecommunications mast (ignore a signed path on the left here used by the *South Cheshire Way*). Af-ter about 50 yards turn left onto a rough access road with cottages on either side and continue to Congleton Road. Turn left and walk along the road.

This lane straddles the county boundary between Chesh-ire and Staffordshire and in clear conditions fine views can be enjoyed into both counties. Eastwards the town of Bidulph

The sham ruins at Mow Cop

sits amid the rolling hills of the Staffordshire Moorlands, while to the west you have an aerial view of the Cheshire Plain with the familiar outlines of Jodrell Bank and Beeston Castle being easily identified. Northwards the hills rise quickly to Congleton Edge and Bosley Cloud with the telecommunications tower on Croker Hill in the distance.

The sudden change from the flat expanse of the Cheshire Plain to the higher and more rugged gritstone hills is due to the presence of a fault known as the Red Rock Fault. This runs in a north-south line along the eastern edge of the plain and separates the ancient gritstone from the younger and much softer sandstone of the plain.

After about ½ mile look for the drive to "Corda Well Farm" on the left. Walk down the drive and at the first bend climb a stile directly ahead. The faint line of a raised track can be seen running through a large grazing field now. The right of way follows this track as it bears leftwards half way across the field, then bends right to pass through a gap in the wall. In the following field the track disappears but a faint footpath continues to contour the hillside with the mast on Croker Hill directly ahead. Cross the next stile which is well hidden amongst a group of holly bushes and continue straight ahead in the following field. There are remains of small quarry workings here and again a faint track marking the right of way can be picked out. Just before the final field, look for a stile and small footbridge hidden in the hedge to your left. Walk directly through the following field now to a stile which leads down to the road.

Opposite, the path leads up the bank to a stile to enter fields once again. Bear half-left in the first field and half-right in the second to a stile which is just to the right of the far corner. Beyond the stile bear left for a few yards then right with the fence to your left and look for the stile among hawthorn bushes and trees. A footbridge immediately after the stile leads over a stream and the path now passes through an attractive 'clough' wood carpeted with bluebells in the spring. At the far end of the wood a short enclosed footpath leads into a narrow lane with Hillside Farm to the right. Turn right here and follow the lane to Castle Farm.

Where the lane bends sharp right towards the farm turn sharp left to a gate. Pass through the gate and follow a farm track enclosed by hedges for some distance now.

Where the track bends left there is a junction of paths and a four fingered sign. Continue straight ahead here signposted "Mossley ½ mile" and after the first stile look for a second stile in the hedge on the right. Go over the stile and continue on the opposite side of the hedge (with the hedge on your left) to join a farm track after several hundred yards. Follow the track down to the road beside Edge Hill Farm.

2. Cross the road and take the signed footpath opposite which shortly joins a short access road with a stone terrace to the right. Follow the access road to the A527 and turn right. Walk along the road for about 100 yards to where a signed footpath on the right, immediately after an old brick-built house, rises into fields once again. The right of way keeps left beside the hedge in the first field before bearing left to a stile which leads onto an enclosed path. After a short rise a second stile leads into a sloping field. Rise directly up the bank until a gap in an overgrown stone wall allows you to bear left onto a more obvious footpath. Shortly, this bends right and rises to a stile on the left.

Just before you climb over the stile, look back for a fine view northwards over the rolling contours of Rainow Hill and Bosley Cloud which rise steeply above Timbersbrook. This is a landscape of lush green hill pastures separated by stone walls, hedgerows and deep clough woods, one of which, known as Cheshire Brook, marks the boundary between Cheshire and Staffordshire.

Westwards you can look out over the town of Congleton which, like its northerly neighbour Macclesfield developed around the fortunes of the silk and cotton industries in the eighteenth and nineteenth centuries. Beyond the town you can look out across the northern half of the Cheshire Plain to the outlines of Jodrell Bank and Alderley Edge and further afield to the tower blocks of Manchester and Stockport with the moors of Rivington and Winter Hill in the distance.

From this stile there two paths. Ignore the path to the right which passes along the crest of Congleton Edge, instead, bear half-right towards a holly tree and continue down to a small stile in the fence about 20 yards further on. Walk directly through the centre of the following large field with a young birch wood to the right and in the far corner go through a gate on the left which leads onto a farm track.

3. Where the track bends left to Whitemore Farm, climb over a stile on the right and walk directly up the field for about 50 yards. Turn left as indicated by a waymark and aim for a stile in the wall which leads into Whitemore Wood. Follow the obvious path through the trees for some distance to join a rough access road near a bungalow on the left. Walk up the access road (away from bungalow) which, after a rise becomes metalled and there are cottages on the right. This area is known as Nick i' th' Hill. A little further on, just before the road begins to drop again, bear left onto a well defined signed footpath which takes you over the northern half of Congleton Edge.

Continue down to the road, turn left (ignore the road immediately on the left) and follow Congleton Road back to Mow Cop retracing the outward journey.

Mara Publications

Mara Publications publish a range of local walking books and have the following list to date:

A Walker's Guide to the Wirral Shore Way - ISBN 0 9522409 0 4. This book describes a linear walk of over twenty miles following Wirral's old coastline between Chester and Hoylake.

Circular Walks along the Sandstone Trail - ISBN 0 9522409 2 0. The Sandstone Trail is Cheshire's best known and most popular walking route. This book gives a complete north-south description of the route as well as breaking the trail into 12 circular walks with the casual walker in mind.

Walking in Wirral - ISBN 0 9522409 1 2. A collection of 12 circular walks in Wirral.

Walking in the Clwydian Hills and the Vale of Llangollen - ISBN 0 9522409 3 9. A collection of circular walks in the beautiful hills and valleys of the Welsh borders.

All the above publications are available through bookshops or by post direct from the publisher. Please check prices by telephone before ordering.

Mara Publications

22, Crosland Terrace, Helsby, Warrington, Cheshire. WA6 9LY. Telephone: 01928 723744.